DRAGON DOUGHNUTS

Ciaran Murtagh

Illustrated by
David Hitch

OXFORD

OXFORD
UNIVERSITY PRESS

Great Clarendon Street, Oxford, OX2 6DP,
United Kingdom

Oxford University Press is a department of the University of Oxford.
It furthers the University's objective of excellence in research, scholarship,
and education by publishing worldwide. Oxford is a registered trade mark of
Oxford University Press in the UK and in certain other countries

Text © Ciaran Murtagh 2017

Illustrations © David Hitch 2017

The moral rights of the author have been asserted

First published 2017

British Library Cataloguing in Publication Data
Data available

978-0-19-837729-0

1 3 5 7 9 10 8 6 4 2

Paper used in the production of this book is a natural, recyclable product
made from wood grown in sustainable forests. The manufacturing process
conforms to the environmental regulations of the country of origin.

Printed in China by Leo Paper Products Ltd.

Contents

Chapter 1
Disappearing Doughnuts

King Harold of Sprinkle Top loved doughnuts. He loved them more than just about anything in the world. He loved chocolate doughnuts. He loved jam doughnuts. He loved doughnuts covered in sparkles, sprinkles and stars. He loved blue doughnuts, yellow doughnuts and pink doughnuts. He even loved doughnuts that had nothing special about them at all. So long as it was a doughnut, he would give it a try. They were his favourite royal treat.

Because he was King, Harold had found the best cook in all the land to make him doughnuts every single day. Betty was a doughnut diva! She was a wizard with a whisk and super with sprinkles! When it came to doughnuts no one was better, and she always had a new recipe she wanted Harold to try.

The Super Sprinkly
Custard Creation –
delicious!

The Jolly Jammy
Doughnut Delight –
double delicious!

The Chewy
Chocolate
Toffee
Temptation –
triple delicious!

The only thing Harold loved more than doughnuts was his daughter, Princess Rose. It was her job to fetch the doughnuts from the kitchen and take them to her father. Every day Rose would skip down the castle corridors carrying the doughnuts, and every day the king would tuck in with a big smile on his face.

So long as King Harold got his daily dose of doughnuts, he was happy. And so long as King Harold was happy, the Kingdom of Sprinkle Top was happy too. But then, one disastrous day, the doughnuts disappeared ...

Chapter 2
Who Took the Doughnuts?

The day had started just like any other.
Betty had been working extra hard
on a new batch of doughnuts for the
king. When she finished, she laid the
doughnuts by the window to cool as
usual. However, when Princess Rose
went to fetch them, the doughnuts
were gone.

"The king's doughnuts have
disappeared!" gasped Rose.

"Disappearing doughnuts?" spluttered Betty. "I've never heard anything like it! They must be here somewhere, help me look!"

Betty and Rose searched the kitchen from top to bottom. They checked in cupboards, drawers and under chairs and tables.

They even looked in the sink! The doughnuts were nowhere to be found.

11

When King Harold heard the news, he was shocked. "No doughnuts?" he said in disbelief. "What am I going to do?"

As Princess Rose told him what had happened, he got grumpier and grumpier.

"Someone must have taken them!" he said. "We have to find the doughnut thief!"

King Harold raced through the castle, looking for clues.

He checked Chuckles the Jester for chocolate spread on his fingers. Nothing.

He checked Lady Claudia for icing on her cheeks. Nothing again.

He checked Percy, his bravest knight, for jammy lips. Even more nothing!

The king asked everyone, but nobody had seen the doughnuts. By the time he had finished, he was grumpier than ever.

To make matters worse, King Harold's grumpy mood was starting to affect everyone in the castle. Soon everybody was walking around with a sour face and a heavy heart.

Then Princess Rose had an idea
that might cheer up her father. She
asked Betty to make another batch of
doughnuts. But when Princess Rose went
to collect them from the kitchen, they
had disappeared too. This was a disaster!
Something had to be done.

Chapter 3
Rose's Plan

Rose thought long and hard until she came up with a plan. She and Betty would make the most amazing doughnuts the kingdom had ever seen and leave them out to cool. Then they would hide and see who came to take the doughnuts.

Rose and Betty worked all morning. Rose stirred the doughnut mixture while Betty got out the toppings and then fried the doughnuts in the pan.

When the doughnuts were cooked, Betty and Rose decorated them. Rose covered the doughnuts in sticky icing. Then they added multicoloured sprinkles, chocolate drops and little silver balls. To finish them off, they added a dollop of custard and a squirt of jam. By the time they were done, the doughnuts looked delicious!

Rose carefully laid the doughnuts out to cool. Then she and Betty hid in the larder and waited for the doughnut thief to appear.

They didn't have long to wait. Soon the sound of rushing wind and flapping wings filled the air. Rose and Betty looked at each other. What was making that noise? Rose peeked through a crack in the door. Her eyes grew wide in amazement as a pair of green, scaly nostrils appeared at the window and gave the doughnuts a good sniff. It was a dragon!

Rose watched as the dragon stretched out its long spiky claws, skewered the doughnuts and flew away.

"A dragon is stealing our doughnuts!"
said Rose.

"We must do something!" said Betty.

Rose agreed and she rushed off to find Percy, the king's bravest knight. At first, Percy was only too happy to help. But when he heard about the dragon his lips went dry and he started to shake. Then he suddenly remembered he was helping his mum

rearrange her toothbrush collection.

Rose went to see Chuckles the Jester, but when he heard about the dragon he climbed out the window.

And so it went on. No matter who Rose spoke to, when they heard about the dragon they were suddenly too busy or too scared to help.

This was terrible. If someone didn't stop the dragon taking King Harold's doughnuts, then the whole Kingdom of Sprinkle Top would be grumpy forever! That night when she went to bed, Rose knew exactly what she had to do.

"If nobody else will stop the dragon," she said as she closed her eyes, "I'll do it myself!"

Chapter 4
Follow That Dragon!

The next morning, Rose was up bright
and early. King Harold was not. He had
decided that he was too grumpy to get
up. Rose knew she had to stop the dragon
taking any more doughnuts, and fast!

She went down to the kitchen to
ask Betty to make one more batch of
doughnuts. While Betty was cooking, Rose
went to the stables and spoke to the stable
boy. If she was going to chase a dragon,
she would need a horse and some armour.

The stable boy rummaged in the back of the storeroom and found some rusty armour and a battered old helmet. It wasn't ideal, but it would have to do. Next, the stable boy led a big black horse out of one of the stalls.

"His name is Charger," said the stable boy. Rose looked at the horse and smiled. He was perfect.

Soon Betty's doughnuts were ready and she popped them out to cool. Rose knew that the dragon would be coming to get the doughnuts, so she squeezed into the rusty armour, clambered on to Charger's back and hid in the stable.

As soon as the doughnuts were put out to cool, the sound of flapping wings filled the air. Rose looked up into the sky. There was the dragon! It was heading straight for the doughnuts.

Rose's heart began to thump. This was it! The dragon swooped down, scooped up the doughnuts and took off once again.

"Come on, boy!" said Rose, as she gripped Charger's reins. "There's no time to lose!" Charger galloped out of the stables and over the drawbridge.

The dragon flew high over the castle and out into the countryside. Rose and Charger raced after it. Soon the castle and the town were far behind them. Rose started to get nervous; she had never been far from the castle before. She tried not to be scared as she and Charger squelched across swamps and raced through deep, dark forests.

They chased the dragon across the whole kingdom. They tiptoed across rickety wooden bridges, splashed through fast-flowing rivers and leaped over more fences and hedges than Rose could count. Finally, a mountain loomed in the distance.

The dragon let out an ear-splitting cry and flew towards the mountain, landing at the very top. Rose and Charger raced to the foot of the mountain. The road ended at a tiny path that spiralled up the cliff face like a rocky helter-skelter. Rose looked up and up and up … there was no way Charger could get up there. The path was too narrow. She was on her own.

Rose gave Charger a pat and set off up the path by herself. Soon she was as high as the clouds and Charger seemed to be the size of an ant far below. Eventually, even the tiny path disappeared and Rose was forced to grip the rock face and climb from stone to stone.

The rocks dug into her hands and scratched her fingers, and the armour felt heavy on her back. But Rose was determined. The whole kingdom was depending on her. At long last, Rose realized that she had reached the top.

She pulled herself up over the rocky edge, dusted the dirt from her hands and strode towards the dragon's lair.

Chapter 5
Dragon Babies

Rose held her breath as she watched the dragon sitting in a huge nest made of twigs and lined with bird feathers. The doughnuts were still stuck on its claws. Just as she was thinking about what to do, something strange happened. The nest twitched and three baby dragons peeked out.

Rose watched in delight as the
mummy dragon warmed up the
doughnuts with her fiery breath and
then held them out towards her babies
for their supper. The baby dragons
seemed to love doughnuts almost as
much as King Harold did and soon,
all that was left of the doughnuts
were crumbs.

"So that's why you're taking the
doughnuts," said Rose quietly to herself.

But she must have spoken a little louder than she thought because suddenly, the dragon was staring at her. The dragon's nostrils flared as she marched towards Rose. Rose gulped. She wanted to run, but then she remembered her grumpy father. He was counting on her. In fact, the whole kingdom was counting on her. She needed to stop the dragon taking the doughnuts. But when she looked at the happy little faces of the baby dragons she thought again.
"I can't take the doughnuts from them. What am I going to do?"

The dragon was now right in front of Rose. She could feel the warmth of her fiery nostrils on her cheek, and suddenly she had an idea. Maybe if the dragon *helped to make the doughnuts*, there might be enough for both the dragon and the king.

Bravely, Rose stepped out from behind
the bushes. She explained her idea to
the dragon as best she could, and when
she was finished the dragon smiled and
nodded her head.

Now all Rose needed to do was get back to the castle before her dad got any grumpier. She looked back down the mountain. Getting home was going to take ages. The dragon could see what Rose was thinking. She picked Rose up in one of her talons, popped Rose on her back and swooped into the air, wings flapping.

Rose held on for dear life as the dragon flew down the side of the mountain and on towards the castle. As they passed Charger, Rose gave a little wave and the brave horse followed on behind.

Chapter 6
Delicious Dragon Doughnuts

When Rose and the dragon reached the castle, nobody could believe their eyes. No one had been brave enough to ride on a dragon's back before! King Harold forgot his grumpiness and popped his head out of his window in astonishment.

"Don't be scared!" called Rose. "This is the dragon who's been taking your doughnuts. But I have a plan to make everything better."

The dragon landed outside the kitchen window and Rose hopped off. She ran into the castle kitchen and helped Betty to make a double batch of doughnuts. When they were finished, Betty was worried.

"These doughnuts won't all fit in the pan," she said.

"They're not going in the pan," said Rose.

Instead, she took them outside to where the dragon was waiting. She nodded at the dragon and a plume of fire spurted from her nostrils. The fire cooked the doughnuts in five seconds flat!

"Well I never!" said Betty as she added toppings. "Instant doughnuts! We can make twice as many, twice as quickly!"

"Exactly," said Rose with a smile. "Plenty for Dad *and* for the dragon's babies!"

By the time they were finished, a crowd had gathered. King Harold was right at the front.

"As King," he said, "I think I should be first to taste these dragon doughnuts." He stepped forward, picked one with extra sprinkles and popped it in his mouth. Everyone held their breath as he chewed. What would he think?

"Delicious!" King Harold said as he finished his mouthful. "The best yet!"

The crowd queued up for a taste
and everyone agreed the new dragon
doughnuts were absolutely delicious!
When they had finished, there were
plenty of doughnuts left for the dragon
to take home. There was just one
problem: there was no way she could
carry them all.

Then Rose had another idea.
She popped the
doughnuts on to
the dragon's
horns. This
way she could
carry as many
as she needed.

"Brilliant!" said the king. "Ring
doughnuts! Just as delicious but easier to
transport!"

He popped a couple on his crown and
smiled. He'd never be far from a dragon
doughnut again!

From that day on, the dragon still took the king's doughnuts, but only after she'd helped make enough for everybody first. And to thank her for solving the mystery of the doughnuts, the king had the blacksmith make Rose her own suit of armour, complete with a jousting lance. Rose never did much jousting, but the lance was perfect for carrying delicious dragon doughnuts!

About the author

I'm an author and scriptwriter. *Dragon Doughnuts* is my 28th book and I got the inspiration for the story from my love of dragons and doughnuts. As well as my books for children, I write some of the most popular kids' TV shows on the planet, including *The Amazing World of Gumball*, *Shaun the Sheep*, *Mr Bean* and *The Furchester Hotel*.